GREAT LAKES COMMERCIAL MORTGAGE, LLC

THE APARTMENT OWNER'S GUIDE TO COMMERCIAL

HUD FINANCING

A comprehensive borrower's guide to the benefits and costs of commercial HUD financing. © 2013 James W. Riead

Don't miss this once-in-a-lifetime opportunity to receive interest rates as low as 3% for 35 years.

By

JAMES W. RIEAD

ISBN: 1481986570

ISBN 13: 9781481986571

Library of Congress Control Number: 2013900985
CreateSpace Independent Publishing Platform
North Charleston, South Carolina

Preface

You have only one interest in reading this book, improving and if possibly maximizing your profit from your investment in apartments. There has been no time, perhaps ever, for you to realize the profits from real estate investing that are available to you today. Our objective is to help you accomplish your goals

The Apartment Owner's Guide to Commercial HUD Financing addresses the use of US Department of Housing and Urban Development (or HUD) commercial loans to finance apartment buildings. Consumer HUD Federal Housing Administration loans for single family to four family homes (residential loans) are not addressed herein.

Many seasoned apartment owners have realized great profits through the use of HUD financing. Such financing offers tremendous potential. If you've accumulated a portfolio of apartments, or if you are considering doing so, consider HUD financing among your commercial loan options.

This book addresses the "why's" and "why not's" associated with the use of HUD financing. This is not meant to be a how-to book; therefore, few technical aspects of HUD loan processing will be discussed. Further, this book contains little HUD terminology.

The use of long-term, fixed-rate financing is not simply a matter of selecting loan A versus loan B. Making such financing decisions requires consideration of whether or not your business benefits from the cash-flow stability that comes with long-term, fixed-rate, low-cost financing. Almost every public corporation adopts this approach to business. Some portion of their capital structure is debt. Some portion of that debt—often a large portion—is long-term fixed rate debt.

Whether you're an apartment owner with extensive financing experience or you're considering purchasing your first apartment, this book will be of value. If you are an experienced professional, consider using this book as a checklist or simply as a means to refresh your memory. For those investors with less extensive experience, read this book in its entirety. If you read only a few chapters, you may miss what's most important to you.

Before we begin, I want to address one of the most common misconceptions concerning HUD financing. HUD does not, as a requirement for a HUD-guaranteed loan, require that you rent to or offer preference to low-income residents or those of any racial, ethnic, or religious group. In addition, HUD loans do not limit the rates you can charge or the profit you can realize. These loans are available to for-profit entities as well as nonprofit entities. Any limitations or restrictions that you may be obligated to honor will be a function of a program or law independent of HUD financing. As one example, you may wish to finance a Section 42 Tax Credit property. Section 42 Tax Credit rules are applied by the Internal Revenue Service, applicable statutes, and local government agencies, but not by HUD. If you are not familiar with the Section 42 program, it is a program that offers apartment owners tax credits in exchange for contractually limiting the rents that are charged and limiting rental to only those tenants whose income meets some test or limit. Section 42 is not a HUD program; however HUD will finance these apartments assuming that they otherwise meet HUD's qualifications.

If you wish to know more about the author, James W. Riead, you may find current information on LinkedIn or on the website www.GreatLakesCommercialMortgage.com

Disclaimer

This book is written to help you take advantage of an opportunity that exists right now. The economy is showing signs of gradual mending and as the economy improves, interest rates will go up and this book will become dated day by day. It may well have a shelf life of one, two or three years, maybe a little longer, but it addresses an opportunity that exists now and which will not exist forever.

This book has been neither authorized nor reviewed by HUD. The information presented here is intended to provide business guidance relating to the consideration of HUD resources versus other financing options that may be available to you. This book is neither intended to provide advice regarding how to use HUD's resources nor does it obligate HUD to anything described herein. The interest rates quoted here reflect the approximate interest rates as of the date of this book. Interest rates on HUD loans are set well into the loan process. The rates applied may be different from the rates communicated in this book. No legal advice is offered herein. You, the reader, are strongly encouraged to retain legal counsel at the appropriate point in your decision process. HUD loans include in their expense estimates a payment allowance for legal counsel. The proposal that you receive should you proceed to the first step in a HUD loan application is what HUD refers to as an engagement letter. Unless provisions are made otherwise, this letter will document said allowance for payment of your legal counsel.

The information contained herein is believed to be correct, though it cannot be guaranteed. HUD may change any rule or process at any time, so information that may be correct at the date of this writing may no longer be correct when you pursue a HUD loan. This book is intended to be a business discussion only; it is neither a HUD handbook nor legal advice. This book is written in Wisconsin and addresses Wisconsin business practices. There are material differences in business practices from state to state.

Table of Contents

CHAPTER 1

What is a HUD Commercial Loan?

The US Department of Housing and Urban Development (or HUD) does not make loans. Instead, they facilitate the guarantee of the US government to assure the repayment of your loan.

When you pursue the process of applying for, being approved for, and then closing a HUD loan, you are asking HUD to substitute the full faith and credit guarantee of the US government in place of your own guarantee. This releases you from liability (other than fraud and related obligations). In other words, Uncle Sam steps into your shoes. As a result, the interest rate and terms applied to your loan are not those for which you would qualify in the conventional market. Rather, you pay an interest rate and receive the terms indexed to what Uncle Sam would pay plus a spread (often a very modest spread), resulting in vastly improved financing terms and materially lower interest rates, all to your benefit. This is why great effort is required to document HUD loans. Further, this is why you pay a fee, in part to HUD for its efforts and in part for the guarantee of the US government. HUD has this authority. Fannie Mae and Freddie Mac do not provide the US government's guarantee on loan's processed through those agencies.

The loan itself will be processed jointly by HUD, a direct underwriter, and likely an independent commercial mortgage originator. A direct underwriter is a highly-capitalized lender approved by HUD to process and service HUD loans. An independent commercial mortgage originator, should you chose to use one, plays a role in initiating the loan, providing communication such as this, and then serving as your advocate.

At the loan closing, the direct underwriter will more than likely fund the loan. That organization will then sell the loan to an investor. The investor may be an insurance company, a pension fund, a bank, or another financial institution. The investor, relying on the full faith and credit guarantee of the US government, accepts an interest rate and terms indexed to those realized by the US government for its obligations. The direct underwriter charges a fee for their effort spent locating an investor to purchase the loan and for costs associated with the loan sale. The direct underwriter will service the loan; you will make monthly payments to that organization.

HUD apartment loans can be used for the following: purchase money mortgages, to rehabilitate a commercial building, for a straight refinance, or for new construction. Under specific conditions, HUD loans can be used to refinance an existing loan and to provide additional cash-out to you.

The end result is a mortgage that imposes certain obligations but also offers certain benefits, both of which will be discussed in this book. In many instances, the resulting loan may prove to be the best source of funding available to you. At the time of this writing, 35 year HUD loans carry an interest rate comparable to many 3 year bank notes. Today, this moment, is your opportunity to lock in today's unprecedented interest rates for a long, long time, perhaps for the rest of your active career.

CHAPTER 2

Qualifying Basics

Basic Criteria. HUD finances only apartments (including senior apartments with age limitations), assisted living facilities, nursing homes, related health-care facilities, and mobile home parks. If there is any question as to the eligibility of the property that you're considering, call your commercial mortgage originator. HUD eligibility rules are tight, if your property does not fit these criteria, there is no appeal or alternative process. HUD does not permit charging entrance fees. Some senior housing developments, as well as some assisted-living developments, include entrance fees or other one-time fees with a comparable objective. Such developments are not eligible for HUD loans. HUD does permit complex legal structures, however, such as commercial condominiums. Should you have a project where some portion of the development does not meet HUD's criteria, it may be possible to use a condominium structure or other legal structure to separate the project into entities and finance through HUD only those entities that meet HUD's criteria while looking to other sources of funding for the remaining entities.

Property Size. For HUD purposes, a five-unit building is defined as a multifamily property. The buildings can, however, contain fewer than five units if multiple buildings constitute a singular project. Twenty duplexes developed as a singular rental project, for instance, could be permissible for a HUD loan.

HUD has no formal, minimum loan size. Further, HUD discourages lenders from suggesting that a loan may be too small. But as a practical matter, loans can be too small, particularly if you're financing several small buildings. As another example, a project that includes ten duplexes, with each on a separate platted lot may require an individual appraisal and engineering evaluation for each building. These are fixed costs. In other words, the cost of an appraisal and an engineering evaluation has no correlation with the size of the loan; rather, the cost corresponds to the effort required to document the assets in accordance with HUD's requirement. You may consider a one-million-dollar loan on a twenty-family apartment to be very practical. The costs associated with processing a one-million-dollar loan for ten duplexes, however, may seem grossly unreasonable. Submission of an application for a HUD loan is at your discretion, though you must be aware that the costs associated with processing a HUD loan vary depending on the asset under consideration.

Most of the costs associated with processing a HUD loan are variable costs—one point is assigned for this, while another point is assigned for something else. If you have a relatively new, single building that is simple in its construction and amenities, the loan size may be quite small and a HUD loan can still be practical.

Refinancing. To be eligible for refinancing, otherwise-qualified properties must be three years old as of the date that your HUD application is submitted. From the point of initial contact with your commercial mortgage originator to the point of application submission to HUD, up to six months may have passed. This process may be shortened if all of your documentation in order. We suggest that you start the application process when your property is about two-and-a-half years old. The determination of initial construction completion will be based on occupancy permits or comparable documentation.

In some cases, if you've refinanced your property with cash-out to you, otherwise-eligible properties cannot be processed by HUD until the prior refinancing loan is at least two-years seasoned. As with new construction, the loan's period of aging is determined by the date on which the application is formally submitted to HUD. Again, this could be six months after you make initial contact with your commercial mortgage originator. In this scenario, we suggest starting your HUD loan application about eighteen months into the aging of your current loan.

Loan Fees and Costs. HUD fees and costs fall into five basic categories:

(1) *Third-party costs* including up-front costs such as appraisals, mid-process costs such as surveys, and end-process closing costs such as legal counsel and title costs. The direct underwriter often invites bids for these services (excluding your legal counsel). He or she will discuss each expenditure with you as you approach the applicable step in the process.

(2) *HUD-initiated fees.* Most of these fees are expressed in points and are nonnegotiable. These costs are incurred at various stages between formal loan submission to HUD and loan closing. HUD also charges small fees based on unit count or other criteria. As one example, HUD assesses a mortgage insurance premium paid at loan closing as well as ongoing insurance premiums for the life of the loan.

(3) *Direct underwriter fees.* HUD establishes guidelines for these fees, though the fees are set by the direct underwriter. Your direct underwriter will likely quote these fees in accordance with the size and complexity of your loan. He or she may also take into consideration the sophistication of your operation and the ease or difficulty of working through the loan process. Direct underwriter fees also include fees to place the loan with an investor and fees to process the application. Some portion thereof may be paid

to independent mortgage originators. Such fees will be disclosed by the direct underwriter in the engagement letter.

(4) *Reserves.* Reserve money is set aside in a segregated account for your benefit. Reserves include one-time funds intended to cover specific repairs (if any) and the initial contribution to an ongoing reserve account. While reserve funds are not costs or fees, they are your money; reserves require setting aside cash and must be budgeted as part of the loan process.

(5) *Interest rate commitment fee.* Near the end of the loan process, you'll be required to pay a fee in order to commit to a specific interest rate. You will be given a window of time after the loan has been approved during which to lock in your interest rate. Payment of the fee solidifies this rate. The commitment fee may not be prominently disclosed in your application documents as it is an in-and-out payment. In other words, you will be reimbursed in full for payment of the interest rate commitment fee once you close the loan, approximately thirty to sixty days following payment. Again, though you will be reimbursed for this transaction, you must budget to pay the fee then wait thirty to sixty days for reimbursement.

Subject to the appraised value of your property, the debt service coverage ratio required by HUD, and the loan to value ratio (or LTV) applicable to your loan, the five loan fees above are routinely funded (or refunded) at closing. Once you have an estimate of these fees and other cash commitments, you can then determine which portion must be covered by cash advances. As a ballpark estimate, one-third of the total fees and reserves must be funded in cash by you. This money will then be reimbursed at closing. The remaining two-thirds will be covered through in-and-out transactions at closing. Whether any or all fees are included in your loan depends upon the appraised value of your property, the LTV of the loan, and the costs that must be disbursed. You will be able to estimate these fees as the loan process proceeds.

Operational Costs. In addition to requiring adherence to specified criteria for approving your loan, HUD also requires that you follow certain operational procedures. For instance, you will be required to undergo an annual, certified audit. If you're considering financing for a Section 42 tax credit property or other property subject to extensive government regulation, you may already be completing most of the certified audit documentation. As such, the administrative burden imposed by HUD's audit requirement would be negligible. On the other hand, if you maintain a loose set of books, answer to no one other than the IRS concerning those records, and don't involve a certified public accountant, a small HUD loan may be an impractical option.

Approval. Your broker will likely quote a time frame within which your loan should be processed—ten months, one year, or otherwise. He or she will likely assume that your records and documentation are complete and are readily accessible. He or she will also assume that turnaround time in response to a HUD request will be prompt. If this isn't the case and your records aren't current and readily accessible, and if your staffing does not permit rapid turnaround in response to a HUD request, processing time will take longer. It could take significantly longer.

Effective Interest Rate. When discussing HUD interest rates, be sure that you and the party with whom you're speaking compare apples to apples. In other words, your HUD loan will consist of three ongoing costs:

1) *The investor rate.* This is the interest rate to be paid to the investor that buys your note (this is the rate that you will lock-in just prior to the closing of your loan). The investor may be a bank, an insurance company, or a pension fund, as examples.

2) *Mortgage insurance premium.* This is paid to HUD for the duration of the loan as a premium for the guarantee of the US government.

3) *Servicing fee.* This fee will be paid to the organization that services your loan, likely the direct underwriter with whom you'll be working throughout the loan process.

The sum of these three components is referred to as the all-in interest rate. This is the one rate that really matters to you. (A textbook definition of all-in interest rate includes the amortization of fees. Neither the engagement letter nor the executive summary use this definition.) Of the three components listed above, the servicing fee will more than likely be established in your original engagement letter; this initial fee will more than likely be the final fee applied. HUD does, however, reserve the right to change the cost of insurance and may do so from time to time. An estimated investor rate will be documented in your engagement letter, but be aware that it is only an estimate. The actual investor rate will be set once you lock your interest rate, about one year into the process. Again, the rate that is important to you is the all-in rate. This is the rate that you will pay for thirty-five to forty years (unless you prepay the loan).

CHAPTER 3

HUD Commercial Loan Characteristics

The LTV (loan to value) of the final loan will vary depending upon a number of factors, including your personal definition of LTV. Nonprofits may be entitled to a higher LTV loan than the typical for-profit entity. Apartments can currently be refinanced at 83 percent LTV if there is no cash out or at 80 percent LTV if there is cash out. In general, the LTV will range between 80 and 90 percent depending upon the application specifics.

Defining LTV. HUD permits certain fees to be paid to affiliates of the borrower on loans involving extensive rehabbing or new construction. These fees must be negotiated in relation to a particular project. Development fees, including fees for providing subcontract labor or services, can be paid to the developer or a related party if the developer in fact provides these services and meets HUD's qualification criteria. For example, a particular loan may be 80 percent LTV, but one-half of the twenty percent equity may be sweat equity, not cash. If you look at cash outlay only, you may realize a 90% LTV loan.

New Construction. New construction must be bonded and prevailing wages must be paid. The interest rate established applies to the construction period as well as the permanent financing period. The loan is non-recourse; this applies during the construction period as well. There is no short term construction loan followed by a take-out permanent loan.

Other Equity Contributions. HUD will accept certain funds contributed by others as equity contributions. Among these funds can be tax incremental financing (or TIF) district improvements that are of specific benefit to your property. Grants and secondary loans can also be counted toward the equity contribution. Each of these sources is subject to limitations, though they may have a significant impact on the cash that may be required to contribute as equity.

Interest Rates. As of January 1, 2013, interest rates vary between 3 and 4 percent. (Interest rates for new construction and extensive rehab are around 4 percent.) The rates are fixed for the duration of the loan. The final rate is set near the end of the loan-approval process. Typically, your loan will close in thirty to sixty days from the date of rate lock fee payment.

Amortization. Loans are fully paid off or amortized over the term of the loan, which is usually thirty-five or forty years. (Forty-year loans most often apply for new construction only.) The loan may be amortized over a shorter duration for properties appraised to have a "remaining useful life" of less than forty six years. The HUD-approved appraiser will make this assessment. Your loan will be amortized over a period of 75 percent of the property's useful life. As an example, if the remaining useful life is assessed at forty years, then your loan may be amortized over thirty years (or 70 percent of forty). If you disagree with the useful-life appraisal, discuss this with your Commercial Loan Originator as making such an assessment is a subjective matter.

Nonrecourse. HUD loans are non-recourse loans. This means that the lender cannot go after your home or other assets beyond specified terms in order to receive payment. More importantly, your home is not at risk. Do not underestimate the importance of this provision, especially if you have partners, investors, or heirs. Refer to Chapter 6 for more information. Keep in mind that with conventional loans absent of nonrecourse provisions, partners and investors may be subject to collection, not only for one's equitable share of the allocated liability, but for the total loan amount. On occasion, lenders will pursue the guarantor with the deepest pockets or the most liquid assets without regard to the proportion of equitable liability allocated to that guarantor, HUD's non-recourse provisions prevent that.

A HUD loan will almost certainly include what are called "carve-out provisions" relative to the nonrecourse provisions. These provisions, in particular the wording thereof, may be subject to some negotiation. Carve-out provisions are intended to protect HUD from gross actions by you, such as misallocation of security deposits or reserve account abuse.

Assumable. HUD loans are assumable. This means that the outstanding balance of a mortgage can be transferred, terms intact, from the existing owner to a buyer. This can be very important in estate planning or in structuring the ownership of an entity involving several investors. In the case of estate planning, this provision can provide the vehicle with which to transfer an asset to heirs without violating loan covenants. In the case of multiple investors, this provision can assist with structuring buy-out agreements such that former investors will be released from ongoing liability.

Prepayment. HUD loans have an initial repayment lock-out provision, which is typically three years followed by an annual, step-down prepayment penalty provision (e.g., 7 percent year 3, 1 percent year 10). Loans are generally free of prepayment restrictions after ten years. HUD loans seldom include defeasance or yield maintenance prepayment provisions. A unique feature of HUD loans is that you have a twenty-five- or thirty-year window open for prepayment without penalty as opposed to most loans, which either have a specific balance due date at the end of the loan term, or a two to six-month window for payment at the end of the loan term. The extended window offered by a HUD loan allows you to refinance when it's most advantageous for you. It also minimizes the risk of being forced to refinance in an adverse market.

CHAPTER 4

Maximizing Loan to Value

When considering a HUD loan to finance apartments in particular, you must first address the LTV of the ultimate loan.

If you have existing debt that you wish to pay off, it's critical to receive an adequate loan to do so. For this purpose, debt to be repaid includes a recorded land contract or other acceptable, recorded evidence of an installment sale. HUD will refinance apartments at an LTV of 83 percent if there is no cash–out to you (83% with the funds used to retire debt and to cover costs associated with placing the HUD loan). While both HUD and a conventional lender may approve an 80% LTV loan for example, HUD may appraise your property at a higher value and hence provide you the greater loan amount.

In general, we suggest that HUD apartment loans be at the maximum amount permitted by HUD. HUD interest rates are likely to be the lowest long term rates available to you, so it makes sense to maximize the loan value. The cost to place a HUD loan includes some fixed costs; amortizing these costs over the highest loan amount is a practical approach. HUD loans also include oper-ational paperwork and audit fees, the cost of which is nearly the same regardless of the loan size. Again, this further justifies maximizing your loan amount. If achieving the maximum HUD loan results in a cash-out to you, it's likely that you have more expensive debt secured by other assets that can be retired through the use of these funds, or that you have alternative investments opportunities that will generate a positive return on this surplus cash.

Assuming that you do wish to maximize the loan amount available to you, consider the topics that follow to determine whether or not a HUD loan may help you to achieve your goal.

Appraised Value. HUD appraisals are always conducted by HUD-approved appraisers. Conventional lenders (such as banks, savings institutions, credit unions, or insurance companies) use appraisers of varying designations and qualifications. Though these appraisers may be equally qualified, you will likely see a distinct difference in the approach and in the end results produced by a HUD-approved appraiser relative to other appraisers. HUD appraisal values will almost always be higher than those generated through a conventional lender. (Higher HUD valuations should continue as long as local markets are distorted by short sales and foreclosures. Once this pattern is no longer an issue, the difference in HUD values and conventional appraised values may disappear)

Benefits of Higher Appraisal Value. The receipt of a higher appraisal value can make or break your loan decision. Say your objective is to refinance an existing loan. If your existing loan may be at a higher LTV than conventional lenders will approve, then a HUD loan may be your solution.

Lenders' Risks. Conventional lenders and HUD face entirely different risks when they place a loan on their standard terms. This difference in risk results in taking different approaches to appraisals and loan amounts. As a consequence, HUD appraisers tend to place less emphasis on comparable sales, short sales and foreclosures, and more emphasis on cash flow and the ability of a property to service debt.

Conventional lenders face two risks that HUD does not face. The first risk is loan maturity and/or interest rate adjustment. The second risk is escalation of the lender's cost of funds. Again, HUD faces neither concern.

These risks are interrelated. The conventional lender is very concerned that his or her cost of funds may escalate. If a loan is placed at a fixed rate, say 4 percent, and the lender's cost of funds goes up to 5 percent, then the lender is locked into an ongoing loss. This loss will continue until the loan is repaid or until a higher interest rate is passed on to you. To address this issue, the lender passes the risk on to you, the borrower, by writing the loan for a short period of time (say three years) or by writing the loan for a longer period of time with periodic interest rate escalation provisions written into the note.

In addition, a bank itself may have transaction issues entirely unrelated to you and your loan. This has happened frequently over the past few years. The bank simply may not have the capital or the liquidity to renew your loan. Other lenders in the area may share these same issues. The bank's inability to fund your loan renewal may put you in default should you be unable to find another loan source.

Any one of these issues can arise with a conventional loan. All appraisals consider replacement costs, comparable sales, and some approach to income stream or capitalization. Replacement costs are largely a formality as few properties today are valued at or above replacement cost. That leaves income stream and comparables as the means to determine value. You know how much your rent has increased. As rent increases, so do costs. Real estate gets older every day. Over time, cost increases will accelerate. The escalation of a bank's cost of funds (and the interest rate that you will eventually have to pay), could be many multiples of the potential NOI improvement of your property. For example, say that a bank's cost of funds today is 2 percent. An increase to 3 percent results in a 50 percent increase to the bank. Lenders must pass this cost on to borrowers. It takes a long time for an apartment's NOI to increase by 50%; as a consequence, the NOI generated by your apartments simply cannot increase in proportion to the increase in cost of funds experienced by lenders over time.

Conventional lenders and their appraisers must recognize this probability and, in so doing, they must apply appraisal techniques that minimize the chance of a bank debacle when interest rates rise.

HUD faces no such risks. They write thirty-five- or forty-year, fully-amortizing loans at today's interest rates. There is no bullet maturity and no interest rate adjustment. HUD faces no arbitrary dates three or five years out, at which point a conventional lender would have to reconsider the original, appraised value of your property. If you have a thirty-five-year loan with monthly payments based on an amortization of thirty-five years at 3 or 4 percent interest, then how are you going to fail? Where is HUD's risk?

HUD appraisals, whether by design or by coincidence, rely heavily on cash flow and little on the recent sales, short sales or foreclosures of comparable properties. They do, however, include studies on comparable rents or rates to assure that your cash flow can be maintained. They compare your operating costs to standard operating costs to assure that you've not neglected any cost element. Once assured that a given level of cash flow is secure, their primary valuation approach is to capitalize that cash flow.

As a result of HUD's minimized risks and their approach to property valuation, your property is likely to appraise at a higher value using HUD valuation metrics than it is using your local lender's valuation metrics. Let me repeat, this may be temporary. Once interest rates rise and foreclosures and short sales become non issues, there may be little difference in the approach of HUD appraisers vs. conventional appraisers.

CHAPTER 5

Maximizing Cash Flow

Business operators (or borrowers) often fundamentally disagree on the amortization term of a mortgage. Some borrowers seek to pay off debt as quickly as possible. In so doing, they may voluntarily place themselves in tight cash-flow positions to achieve their pay-off goal. Those who take this approach certainly recognize the costs and risks associated with rapid debt repayment. Use of a long-term HUD loan, however, can minimize such costs. These costs are described further below.

Refinancing with Cash-Out. You may consider equity in your property the same as cash, that isn't the case. You may also consider the equity in your property available to fund major repairs or other unexpected incidents, but that is also not necessarily the case. It can be very difficult to refinance a property to pull cash out. Lenders may question your reasons for so doing and refuse the loan. If you are approved, your interest rate is likely to be higher for a cash-out than for a straight refinance. Further, the lender may put the cash-out loan on a shorter amortization and/or a shorter maturity. Equity is equity, but equity is not cash. A long-term amortization loan (especially around 3 or 4 percent) should allow your property to generate significant, free cash flow. A long term amortizing mortgage will result in a higher level of debt at any given moment, but it also means that you will have more cash on hand.

Risk of Default. A loan on a fifteen-year amortization versus a thirty-year amortization (all other factors being equal) will result in less available cash to cushion a rainy day. Should something happen—major damage that requires significant repair, a disruption in occupancy—your risk of loan default is much higher. The year 2013, the time of this writing, brings very unusual times. Money is almost free. At this point, there exists almost no opportunity cost associated with withdrawing cash. Money costs only 3 or 4 percent. A host of opportunities are available for reinvestment of these funds.

If interest rates were 8 percent, for example, paying down debt might seem like an obvious choice. Today, however, that's not the case. Today it might seem more reasonable to borrow as much as possible at the existing, low rates, then paying that loan off as slowly as possible, assuming that your underlying business is sound.

CHAPTER 6

The Value of Non-recourse Financing

Having non-recourse financing may improve your overall credit standing in the eyes of other lenders. As lenders consider your global cash flow, they will analyze your upcoming debt maturities, each of which poses some risk to your financial strength. You may not be able to renew these notes, for instance, or one of the lenders who holds a note that may soon come due may be irrational and do something to impair your credit. If the upcoming renewals are nonrecourse notes, your equity is at risk, but your other assets are not at risk, the lender is not going to be able to run around slapping judgments on everything you own.

Now to the mechanics of non-recourse debt. HUD financing offers many benefits, chief among which are long-term amortization (resulting in low monthly payments with no interest rate escalation exposure) and nonrecourse financing. The lender still has recourse, though it is limited to taking possession of the asset.

By custom, many lenders and many borrows don't give recourse any consideration. It is assumed that you, the borrower, will personally guarantee any debt. It's very possible that you have already signed a mortgage note without giving this matter much or any consideration.

This is an area where you, as the borrower, require legal advice. This book is not intended to provide legal advice. As borrowers have grown accustomed to signing personally and placing this provision in notes has become routine, it may have never occurred to you to question this matter. From the outset, the standard approach sounds fair. You want to borrow the money and you will ultimately control the asset, so why would you not be liable for repayment in full?

Be aware, however, that the playing field is far from level. The lender holds all the cards. The lender has full recourse; you possess no offsetting rights. The potential issues described below are subject to the enabling provisions present in your note. More than likely, they're already there.

As a practical matter, the property cannot be passed on to your heirs upon your death if your personal guarantee is a condition of the loan. Your heirs can inherit the property, but they may be forced to refinance or sell it under duress. Non-recourse provisions make this inheritance little more than a clerical matter.

If you have partners you may be held individually liable. This provision can make the dissolution of a partnership next to impossible. Also in the case of partnerships, the lender may select you as the party from which to collect. This forces you to go after your partners in pursuit of reimbursement.

Should the investment go wrong for any reason, the lender may skip foreclosure and take action against your personal guarantee. The property remains subject to the obligations of the mortgage, but the lender may pursue a personal judgment and docket it against everything you own, including your home.

The loan may also contain default provisions that you've not considered. For example, the lender may appraise your property from time to time over the term of your loan using their criteria for property valuation. The lender may require that your cash flow maintain a specific DSCR. Remember, the lender writes and enforces their rules. If the property's reappraisal results in an insufficient loan to value, or debt service coverage ratio, this could trigger a default. If your note includes enabling language, then you could personally be held liable. You do not have to miss a mortgage payment to be held in default.

During the initial loan process, you likely provided your conventional lender with financial information on your property. You probably calculated what you considered to be key ratios, assuming that the lender used those same ratios to make their loan decision. This may not have been the case. Your conventional lender may have done their own calculations and used their own internal criteria without disclosing as such to you. Vacancies, unexpected expenses, or other factors could therefore put your loan in violation of the lender's Criteria. You might have no way of foreseeing such issues.

In today's world of overextended federal, state, and local budgets, you may be exposed in ways that you could not have imagined. You may count on government reimbursement or other payments as a fundamental part of your business; those payments could fall months behind. This scenario may place you in default on your mortgage and facing personal deficiency.

A competitor may irrationally build a project in head-to-head competition with yours, taking you both down.

Non-recourse provisions cannot address all of the issues mentioned above. But HUD gives you the opportunity to actively involve your own counsel in drafting these provisions and providing you with legal advice. Your legal fees are considered part of the expense of the loan. The HUD loan requires you to retain liability for certain items, a scenario referred to as a carve-out. You will likely be responsible for maintaining security deposits and will be held liable for any shortfall. You will also be held liable for any shortage in operational or reserve accounts.

Again, this book is intended to open discussion for certain business considerations; it is not intended to proffer legal advice. As a practical business matter, non-recourse provisions drafted with your counsel can be crucial to the long-term success of your business enterprise.

CHAPTER 7

Resale

As discussed earlier, frequent objections to the consideration of HUD financing relate to a fear of HUD's dictating rents, or profits, or the nature of tenants who may rent the property, none of these concerns are real. The second frequent objection is that the owner may wish to sell the property in a few years and that the HUD loan will inhibit if not prohibit that sale. There are many facets to this issue.

First, HUD loans are assumable, so a HUD loan does not prohibit a sale. The real issues are the consequences to the fixed interest rate and of prepayment penalties

First, the consequences of fixed interest rates. Had you placed a HUD loan during a period of high interest rates, say at an interest rate of 8%, and if you wished to sell that property today when rates are about 3%, such a HUD loan would certainly inhibit your sale, no one would want to assume that 8% loan.

But interest rates are not 8 percent today; they are about 3 or 4 percent. The odds are that if you enter into a 35 year HUD loan at 3% today that at some point during the 35 year term interest rates will be higher than those that you are obligated to pay. When interest rates move up lenders tend to restrict fund availability as they do not want to make a loan at an interest rate that is lower than the rate that they will charge tomorrow. Higher interest rates can be coupled with restricted mortgage money availability.

Should you wish to enter into a HUD loan at about 3% and should you wish to sell at a point in time when interest rates are about 3%, your HUD loan is neutral in terms of interest rates, but it does provide a floor on value and provides the potential buyer with the benefit of knowing that the property has been through a HUD valuation review and through HUD inspections.

Should you decide to sell at a point in time when market interest rates are 5%, you have the ability to not only sell your real estate but to effectively sell your mortgage as well. Should your potential buyer intend to hold the property for 10 years, and should assuming your HUD loan save that buyer 2% a year for 10 years, or 20% over that term, assuming that loan has value to that buyer. The buyer will pay a premium to be able to assume this loan.

Should you wish to sell in a period when mortgage money is tight, which it is from time to time; you have the benefit of being able to sell when no one else can sell. Buyers who are then in the market will have little choice but to negotiate with you.

The bottom line is that over time, and from time to time, owning a property with a low interest rate assumable mortgage can aid you in your ability to sell, and it can add value to the sale as the interest rate differential, the savings resulting from assuming your mortgage relative to entering into a higher market rate mortgage, can add to the value of the transaction.

Then there is the issue of the prepayment penalty. Most longer term loans have a prepayment penalty, usually defeasance of yield maintenance. Most long term loans allow repayment without penalty only at the end of the term of the loan, sometimes only on the specific date of loan maturity, sometimes within a window of two to six months at the end of the loan term. If you wish to sell with the buyer providing his/her own financing, or if you wish to refinance during the term when these penalty provisions are in place, the penalties can be severe, easily hundreds of thousands of dollars.

HUD loans offer two distinct advantages. First, they have a step down penalty which can be much more modest that yield maintenance or defeasance. Second, HUD has a window for repayment without penalty starting at year ten and lasting for the remaining duration of the loan. A 35 year loan has a 25 year window open for repayment without penalty. HUD loans offer you much more flexibility than loans offered by most other sources.

CHAPTER 8

The Application Process

Once you've made the decision to finance a property through HUD, you will begin the application process, which is likely to take at least eight months. The application process, both time-consuming and effortful, will require you to make financial commitments and cash contributions at several points throughout.

This chapter contains no discussion of forms or technical elements of the application process. Rather, it is intended to provide an overview, highlighting critical points that deserve particular attention.

The first step is to discuss the loan with your commercial loan originator. Ask him or her to provide you with an executive summary prepared by the direct underwriter of his, her, or your preference. This step is free and takes very little time. You may receive the document on the same day that you provide the necessary data.

Once you have the executive summary, meet with your commercial mortgage originator and go over the document step-by-step, comparing it with your objectives. Consider every detail therein, but pay critical attention to the net cash proceeds amount. If your objective is to refinance a loan for three million dollars, for example, or to finance a purchase with a three-million-dollar loan, or if you seek a specific cash-out amount, the executive summary might indicate that any of these goals could be tight. If you're concerned about cash proceeds, look into this more deeply before you proceed. If you're refinancing or purchasing an older property that may be somewhat functionally obsolete or suffer from deferred maintenance, be sure that these issues are addressed before you spend money on an appraisal.

The second step is to request an engagement letter. This document will be provided free of charge, but requires a deposit should you elect to execute. The engagement letter will include a copy of the executive summary (updated with any corrections) as well as a more complete description of the loan application process. The engagement letter is a legal document. Consider asking counsel to review it prior to your execution thereof or payment of any deposit.

The process typically calls for ordering an appraisal at this point, but that may not be the best course of action. Plan to discuss at least the following two issues with the direct underwriter and his or her staff in their offices. We do encourage you to do this, and to meet the staff, as they want the loan to proceed and meet your objectives, and they may bring up issues that you never considered.

First, discuss sending more complete financial information to the direct underwriter for their feedback regarding the condition of your documentation. Doing so will also allow the direct underwriter and your commercial mortgage originator to better estimate your property's appraised value. Now is the time to find out if your records don't meet necessary standards and require updates. You must be confident that your documentation will be up to par as the formal HUD appraisal has a shelf life of only four months once complete and signed. If your records are lacking, or if your clerical staff has difficulty satisfying information requests in a timely matter, now is the time to make changes. If your application isn't complete and ready to submit to HUD within the four-month window following the date of the appraisal, you may need to pay for an update of your appraisal.

Second, discuss with the direct underwriter whether the engineering study should be conducted before the appraisal is conducted (the engineering study addresses the physical condition of your property and may call for expensive repairs that must be made as a condition of the loan). He or she will advise you as to which assessment (appraisal or engineering study) provides the greatest risk. We suggest addressing the greater risk first. If the condition or the design of the property may be a material issue, for instance, we suggest ordering the engineering study before the appraisal.

The third step of the loan application process is the appraisal. Look at the appraiser's estimate of the property's remaining useful life. If this loan is for new construction, then remaining useful life should not be an issue. But if the loan is for an existing property, be sure that the loan amortization meets your objectives. As discussed previously, HUD sets the loan term at 70 percent of the asset's useful life, which equates to a loan term of thirty-five years if the property has a fifty-year remaining useful life. Alternatively, if the appraiser concludes that the property has a forty-year remaining useful life, then HUD will set the loan amortization at twenty-eight years. This may be fine with you. If it's not and you don't challenge the assessment at this point in the process, it may be too late once the direct underwriter makes the formal HUD submission.

Step four is submission of the loan application to HUD. The few weeks prior to formal submission by your direct underwriter, you will be requested to provide or verify a host of documents and data. You may need copies of insurance policies, occupancy permits, documentation of your current debt, and so forth. Your appraisal cannot be more than four months old at the point of formal submission to HUD or it will need to be updated. When verifying facts and gathering supporting documentation, time is of the essence.

At step five, you will meet with the local HUD office, either face-to-face or over the phone. We suggest meeting in person. This meeting can take place either before or after your loan application has been formally submitted. The primary purpose is to evaluate your management, which is really an evaluation of intangibles.

You'll also meet some of the key people involved in processing your loan as well as those who will be reviewing your annual audits. At the end of the exchange, you should be "invited" to make your loan submission to HUD.

Next, you will interact with HUD through your direct underwriter. It may be a month or more before you get any feedback depending on the number of loan applications in the HUD office and to be processed before yours.

Step seven consists of loan approval and documentation. Your legal counsel will work with HUD's counsel to draft the final loan documents, during which you will participate.

Your interest rate will be finalized at step eight. Once the loan is approved and the supporting documentation is nearly complete, you will be given a window of time in which to lock in the interest rate. Doing so requires payment of a rate-lock fee, which will be refunded to you at the loan closing.

The next step, step nine, is drafting the closing documents and the loan closing.

CHAPTER 9

HUD vs. Conventional Loan Considerations

The selection of any lender and any specific loan program involves many elements. To properly evaluate HUD as an option, you must first address your alternatives. It is especially helpful to compare potential program options head-to-head. In most cases you're most viable longer term funding option will be Fannie Mae or Freddie Mac, so we will pay particular attention to this comparison. Below are specific considerations that you may wish to format as a check list.

1) Fannie Mae/Freddie Mac. If you are considering the use either of these funding sources, please continue to complete this section. In a nutshell, the loan term for either will be no more than ten years (their longer terms rates are not likely to be competitive with HUD). You will have a bullet loan with a very short window for prepayment of 2 to 6 months at the end of the loan term. You will also have either defeasance or yield-maintenance prepayment penalties, which are vastly more severe than HUD's step-down prepayment penalty. HUD will offer you a twenty-five-year window in which to repay your loan with

no penalty. This will essentially allow you to pick your own, optimum repayment timing. Fannie Mae and Freddie Mac loans are not guaranteed by the US Government and tend to be rate competitive with HUD only for shorter duration loans. Pay particular attention to the prepayment penalties. HUD's step penalty lets you know what the penalty will be, for example 2% in year 8, or $200,000 on a ten- million-dollar loan. Defeasance or yield maintenance, with 2 years remaining on a ten- million -dollar ten year loan, can be $700,000. HUD, Fannie Mae and Freddie Mac are all assumable. But if you are considering refinancing the property, or selling it and paying off the loan, in a period with 1, 2, or 3 years left on the term of the loan, HUD is by far your best option. The prepayment penalties under a HUD loan are likely to be a fraction of the prepayment penalties under either Fannie Mae or Freddie Mac.

2) Insurance Company Funding. If you opt for an insurance company loan, again, please still complete the checklist. Insurance company loans include a much shorter amortization period as well as a defeasance or yield-maintenance prepayment penalty. Insurance company loans are most appropriate for NNN leased properties, warehouses, and a number of commercial operations, but are seldom the best choice for apartments. Insurance company loans are typically non-recourse and assumable, and are typically for a term of 10 years or more. Apartments will not typically generate enough cash flow to support their amortization

3) Will the apartments qualify for a HUD loan? The principal issues are the type of property, the age of the property (if it was recently constructed), and the aging of the current debt if it was refinanced with cash-out within the past two years. If you're unable to answer these questions, speak with your mortgage broker.

4) Is repaying a current loan, or closing the purchase of a property important to you? If so, keep in mind that HUD

loans require significant processing time. This problem can be alleviated, however, by starting the process early. Will the HUD loan generate the proceeds needed to repay the existing loan? HUD will process an apartment refinancing at 83 percent LTV. For this purpose, a land contract or other recorded instrument documenting an installment sale will qualify as existing debt. HUD's appraisal will likely reflect a higher value than the assessed value provided by a typical, conventional lender's appraisal, but again processing time is a big issue

5) Is the loan large enough to justify the fees and costs?

6) Is the property in a condition such that costs should be minimal? Is it a single building or many small buildings? Is it in good condition or will getting approval prove to be difficult? Consider the cost of appraisals and engineering studies as well as the reserves potentially required from the mortgage proceeds.

7) Do you currently have your books reviewed or certified by a CPA and will meeting HUD's reporting requirements involve minimal effort? This would likely be the case for a Section 42 property, Section 8 property, or a co-owned property whose investors receive periodic reports.

8) How much value do the nonrecourse provisions of a HUD loan offer you? These provisions may be of little value if you own the property in your name alone and the loan will be low in relation to the property's value. Non-recourse provisions will be much more valuable if you have investors or partners; if passing the property to heirs during the term of the loan is a realistic possibility; if you may want to sell the property subject to the loan and have no continuing liability; if the amount of debt is very large relative to your total net worth; or if the risks associated with new construction or major rehabilitation are involved.

9) What are your amortization alternatives? HUD's typical thirty-five or forty-year amortization schedules may significantly increase your cash flow, particularly if your alternatives are fifteen, twenty, or twenty-five-year options. Improved cash flow not only puts more cash in your pocket, it also greatly reduces default risk as your payments are less than they would be on a shorter term amortization mortgage.

10) What is the interest rate differential? For the first three years, the differential may be minimal. HUD may be 3 percent and your bank may offer you a 3 percent, three-year note. If your bank wanted to loan you money for thirty-five years, they would. Instead, your bank wants the freedom to demand that you repay the loan and the freedom to raise your interest rate. They want to be able to shift the interest rate risk to you. What value do you place on this?

11) Do you want to sell in the next few years? Many property owners decline HUD loans as they intend to sell in three, four, or five years. We would suggest that this is in fact the reason that you want a HUD loan, particularly a high-LTV HUD loan. HUD loans are assumable; the interest rate is not subject to escalation on assumption. If you have a 3 percent loan and market interest rates are 5 percent when you wish to sell, your loan will add significant value and liquidity to your property. This is very likely to be the case for HUD loans placed now, over the next decade or so interest rates are likely to go up and the loan is likely to add value to your property.

12) Will this be a large loan? Is the loan material relative to your net worth? If this loan will be very large relative to your net worth the non-recourse provisions could save you from bankruptcy should the property fail to meet your obligations.

CHAPTER 10

Potential Issues

Most of the issues covered in this chapter have been discussed at other points in the book. Regardless, we will point them out again as they can be irritants during the loan decision and application process.

- If you finance through HUD, you will need an annual audit signed by a CPA. This may or may not be an expense that you will incur with the other lenders that you may be considering.

- If you finance through HUD, you can withdraw cash, what HUD calls "surplus," only once or twice a year. The audit will specify the approved withdrawal amount.

- If you finance through HUD, you will be entitled to withdraw a management fee as an ongoing expense of the entity (if you manage it), but the amount will be as agreed upon by you in covenants regulating the loan.

- If you finance through HUD, you will need to make a substantial deposit to lock the interest rate. This fee will be refunded at loan closing, likely within thirty to sixty days of making the deposit. Be certain to budget for this expense, however, as payment thereof often creeps up on borrowers.

- The HUD appraisal is only good for four months from the date that the appraiser physically inspects your property. These four months can move very quickly and all documentation must be completed within this time frame. If the loan is not submitted to HUD within the four-month period (barring an extension granted by HUD), you will have to pursue and pay for an updated appraisal. Be sure to remain in close contact with the direct underwriter during the appraisal process. It is very important that the appraiser not visit your property prematurely as the date of his or her visit will start the four-month timer for HUD loan submission.

- You will be required to maintain an interest-free reserve account for major repairs. This should not be a burden as the reserve is intended to pay for repairs; it is not money intended to sit in the bank.

- You must form a single-purpose entity to own the property.

- Net leases are very difficult to structure and to be approved by HUD, although it can be done. The tenant and the landlord, however, must both be subject to HUD covenants. Cash payments to both are governed by those covenants.

GLOSSARY

While we've made every effort to avoid so-called HUD speak, there are a few necessary terms included with which you may be unfamiliar. Those terms are defined here taking into consideration the context in which they are used in this book.

"All In" Interest Rate: The sum of the interest rate paid to the investor, the mortgage insurance premium paid to HUD along with each mortgage payment, and the service fee paid to the organization that services the mortgage. A textbook definition would include the amortization of fees. That's difficult to do, however, for comparative purposes as short-term loans require periodic loan renewals or refinancing which require repeat appraisals, fees, and perhaps title costs at each renewal.

Amortization: The period of time over which payments of principal and interest are paid down. A loan may have a ten-year term, but the monthly payments may be made on the basis of a thirty-year term. The result would be a significant, remaining balance in principal when the loan is due in ten years.

Carve-Outs: A non-recourse loan retains certain personal liabilities. Those liabilities that remain your responsibility, and for which the lender may be able to pursue you personally, are routinely referred to as carve-outs

Cash-Out: As used in this book, the funds remaining after paying off an existing mortgage with a new mortgage. The excess in funds provides the borrower with a cash-out, or available cash after retiring the original debt. In general, loans with cash-out to the borrower are considered less desirable than loans with no cash-out. Such loans may be assigned less favorable terms in comparison to loans with no cash-out option. HUD does permit cash-out, to an LTV of 80%, for apartments.

Commercial Loan Originator: This term is often used interchangeably with commercial mortgage broker, though they don't have the same meaning. A commercial mortgage originator, who may or may not be independent of a major financial institution, is responsible for initiating a mortgage loan submission and serves as your advocate through the process.

Conventional Loan: As used in this book, a loan funded by a bank, savings institution, insurance company, or credit union.

Department of Housing and Urban Development (or HUD): Established in 1965, the U.S. federal department that administers federal programs dealing with better housing and urban renewal.

Direct Underwriter: As used in this book, a financial institution with a contractual relationship with HUD, Fannie Mae, or Freddie Mac, who has the authority to underwrite loans to the respective institution's specifications and with the authority and means to fund those loans at the loan closing.

Engagement Letter: A document prepared by a direct underwriter that establishes the terms of a proposed HUD loan, which, if executed by the proposed borrower, becomes the initial contract engaging the direct underwriter to process a HUD loan. Conventional lenders write a Terms Sheet to serve this same purpose, however the Terms Sheet may or may not become a contract upon its execution.

Executive Summary: A summary prepared by a direct underwriter, typically two pages in length, which is based solely upon financial data and information data initially provided by the applicant. The document summarizes the amount of a loan, approximate interest rate and amortization, costs to process the loan, and other statistical data pertaining to a proposed loan. The executive summary is considered a preliminary document as the loan will be based up the appraisal and other documents submitted during the process of approving the loan.

Fannie Mae: The Federal National Mortgage Association (FNMA) commonly referred to as Fannie Mae, which was founded in 1938 during the Great Depression.

Freddie Mac: An organization chartered by Congress in 1970 to provide liquidity, stability, and affordability to the nation's housing market.

Free and Clear (or F&C): A property with no recorded debt.

Insurance Company Funding: As used here, commercial real estate loans funded by the real estate lending department of an insurance company.

Investor: As used here, the organization that provides the permanent funds for a HUD-guaranteed mortgage. Funds at loan closing may be provided by the investor or by the direct underwriter (HUD does not fund the mortgage)

Loan to Value (or LTV): A ratio calculated by the amount of the loan divided by the value of the asset.

Mortgage Insurance Premium: The cost of HUD insurance provided on a HUD-guaranteed loan. There are two premiums associated with each loan: an initial premium paid at loan closing and an ongoing premium paid with each mortgage payment.

Net Operating Income (or NOI): The income generated by a commercial property after the payment of all operation expenses, management fees, taxes including real-estate taxes, and reserves funding as may apply to a given loan (if there is one), but prior to debt service and non-cash items such as amortization and depreciation. This is the number typically used to value real commercial real estate according to income capitalization.

Non-recourse: A state in which the mortgage lender does not have the legal right to collect on the borrower's personal assets as a consequence of the failure of a business financed by a loan.

Tax Incremental Finance District (or TIF District): An area of land to which a special tax provision is applied. This particular term is used in Wisconsin, though other states likely have similar acronyms for comparable government action. Under the terms of a TIF, a municipality may make cash payment to the developer of property within the TIF district, may provide infrastructure, such as roads, sewers, or parking structures, or they may waive real estate taxes charged to the developer all on the premise that the proposed development will ultimately reimburse the municipality through increased economic activity. HUD can recognize value created by a TIF district and a TIF contract relative to a specific property, and that value can be credited to equity under specific circumstances.

Terms Sheet: A document prepared by a lender such as Fannie Mae, Freddie Mac, a conduit, or an insurance company that outlines the terms of a proposed loan. The term is effectively interchangeable with engagement letter, though the latter has a more structured format.

www.ingramcontent.com/pod-product-compliance
Lightning Source LLC
Chambersburg PA
CBHW051255170526
45165CB00004B/1717